09
1/11   10
         1/1

8/04

Allosaurus

by Daniel Cohen

Consultant:
Brent Breithaupt
Director
Geological Museum
University of Wyoming

Bridgestone Books
an imprint of Capstone Press
Mankato, Minnesota

Bridgestone Books are published by Capstone Press
151 Good Counsel Drive, P.O. Box 669, Mankato, Minnesota 56002
http://www.capstone-press.com

Library of Congress Cataloging-in-Publication Data
Cohen, Daniel, 1936–
    Allosaurus / by Daniel Cohen.
    p. cm.—(Discovering dinosaurs)
    Summary: Briefly describes how this dinosaur looked, what it ate, where it lived, and how
scientists learned about it.
    Includes bibliographical references and index.
    ISBN 0-7368-1618-6 (hardcover)
    1. Allosaurus—Juvenile literature. [1. Allosaurus. 2. Dinosaurs.] I. Title.
QE862.S3 C548 2003
567.912—dc21   2002010445

Editorial Credits
Erika Shores, editor; Karen Risch, product planning editor; Linda Clavel, series designer;
    Patrick D. Dentinger, cover production designer; Angi Gahler, production artist; Alta
    Schaffer, photo researcher

Photo Credits
Cheryl R. Richter, 8
Corbis/Richard Cummins, 4
Edward Rasmussen, University of Wyoming Photo Service, 18
The Natural History Museum/J. Sibbick, 12
Patrick D. Dentinger, cover, 1
Photophile, 10; Richard Cummins, 14
Tom Stack & Associates/Tom & Therisa Stack, 16
Visuals Unlimited/Ken Lucas, 6

1 2 3 4 5 6 08 07 06 05 04 03

Table of Contents

Allosaurus 5

The World of Allosaurus 7

Parts of Allosaurus 9

Relatives of Allosaurus 11

A Time of Giants 13

What Allosaurus Ate 15

Hunters and Scavengers 17

End of Allosaurus 19

Discovering Allosaurus 21

Hands On: Hunting in a Pack 22

Words to Know 23

Read More 24

Internet Sites 24

Index 24

Allosaurus compared to a 5-foot-tall (1.5-meter-tall) human

Allosaurus

Allosaurus (AL-loh-SORE-us) was a large, meat-eating dinosaur. Its name means "strange reptile." An adult Allosaurus was about 39 feet (12 meters) from its nose to the end of its tail. It stood 12 feet (3.7 meters) tall and weighed about 2 tons (1.8 metric tons).

The World of Allosaurus

Allosaurus lived about 150 million years ago. Earth looked different during the time of Allosaurus. Earth's landmasses were closer together. The climate was warm and wet. Giant ferns, gingkos, and other tropical plants covered the land.

tropical
anything related to warm and wet weather

head

tail

legs

Parts of Allosaurus

Allosaurus had a long, narrow head. Two small horns stuck out from its head. Curved teeth filled its mouth. Allosaurus had large claws. It stood on strong hind legs. Its tail helped it balance when it ran.

Dilophosaurus was a relative of Allosaurus. Both Allosaurus and Dilophosaurus were theropods.

Relatives of Allosaurus

Allosaurus belonged to a group of dinosaurs called theropods. Many theropods lived during the time of dinosaurs. Dilophosaurus (die-LOF-oh-SORE-us) was a theropod. Its name means "two-crested reptile." It had two crests on its skull.

crest
a flat, bony plate on the top of a dinosaur's head

A Time of Giants

Allosaurus shared Earth with some of the largest land animals ever to live. These plant-eating dinosaurs were the sauropods (SORE-oh-pods). Diplodocus (dip-LOH-doh-cus) and Brachiosaurus (BRAK-ee-oh-SORE-us) were two large sauropods.

What Allosaurus Ate

Allosaurus was a carnivore. It may have eaten sauropods and other dinosaurs. Some scientists think Allosaurus hid until prey came near. Allosaurus would attack and slash prey with its sharp claws and teeth. Allosaurus used its powerful jaws and sharp teeth to kill its prey.

Hunters and Scavengers

Allosaurus may have hunted in a pack. A group of Allosaurus could attack and kill a large dinosaur such as Diplodocus. Some scientists think Allosaurus was a scavenger. It would find and eat dinosaurs that were already dead.

scientist
a person who studies the world around us

17

End of Allosaurus

Allosaurus became extinct about 135 million years ago. New dinosaurs appeared. Some of the new meat-eaters were larger than Allosaurus. Many of the new plant-eating dinosaurs were smaller and faster than the giant sauropods.

extinct
no longer living anywhere in the world

Montana

South Dakota

Wyoming

Utah Colorado

UNITED STATES

Oklahoma

New Mexico

☐ Areas where Allosaurus
fossils have been found

Discovering Allosaurus

The first Allosaurus fossils were discovered in Colorado in 1869. Othniel Charles Marsh first named Allosaurus in 1877. People have found more than 60 complete Allosaurus skeletons in North America. The most complete skeleton was found in northern Wyoming.

Hands On: Hunting in a Pack

Some scientists think Allosaurus hunted together in packs. A large dinosaur such as Diplodocus would have been difficult for one Allosaurus to kill. But many Allosaurus could attack and kill a Diplodocus. Try this activity to learn how Allosaurus may have hunted.

What You Need

A large room
Four or more players
1 apple, 1 orange, and 1 banana
Stopwatch

What You Do

1. Choose one player to be the Allosaurus and one player to be the timekeeper. The Allosaurus leaves the room.
2. The timekeeper hides the apple, orange, and banana in different places throughout the room.
3. The Allosaurus enters the room. The timekeeper starts the stopwatch.
4. The Allosaurus searches for the apple, orange, and banana. When the Allosaurus finds all the fruit, stop the stopwatch. How long did it take for the Allosaurus to find the fruit?
5. Now, have three players search for the fruit. Repeat steps 2–4. Did the group of Allosaurus find the fruit faster?

Words to Know

balance (BAL-uhnss)—to try to keep steady without falling

carnivore (KAR-nuh-vor)—an animal that eats meat

climate (KLYE-mit)—the usual weather in a place

dinosaur (DYE-na-sore)—an extinct land reptile; dinosaurs lived on Earth for more than 150 million years.

extinct (EK-stingkt)—no longer living anywhere in the world

fossil (FOSS-uhl)—the remains or traces of something that once lived; bones and footprints can be fossils.

reptile (REP-tile)—a cold-blooded animal with a backbone; scales cover a reptile's body.

scavenger (SKAV-uhn-jer)—an animal that looks through waste for food

Read More

Cole, Stephen. *Allosaurus!: The Life and Death of Big Al.* New York: Dutton Children's Books, 2001.

Goecke, Michael P. *Allosaurus.* Dinosaurs. Edina, Minn.: Abdo, 2002.

Wilson, Ron. *Allosaurus.* Dinosaur Library. Vero Beach, Fla: Rourke, 2001.

Internet Sites

Track down many sites about Allosaurus.
Visit the FACT HOUND at *http://www.facthound.com*

IT IS EASY! IT IS FUN!

1) Go to *http://www.facthound.com*
2) Type in: 0736816186
3) Click on "FETCH IT" and FACT HOUND will find several links hand-picked by our editors.

Relax and let our pal FACT HOUND do the research for you!

Index

carnivore, 15

claws, 9, 15

climate, 7

Colorado, 21

crests, 11

Earth, 7, 13

extinct, 19

fossils, 21

horns, 9

Marsh, Othniel Charles, 21

packs, 17

plants, 7

prey, 15

sauropods, 13, 15, 19

scavenger, 17

tail, 5, 9